彩虹桥 汉语分级读物
Rainbow Bridge Graded Chinese Reader

Level 1

GW00481052

Magical Lotus Lanterns

宝莲灯

刘菊 改编

MP3
Download Online
www.sinolingua.com.cn

华语教学出版社
SINOLINGUA

First Edition   2016
Second Printing   2017

ISBN 978-7-5138-0989-4
Copyright 2016 by Sinolingua Co., Ltd
Published by Sinolingua Co., Ltd
24 Baiwanzhuang Road, Beijing 100037, China
Tel: (86) 10-68320585   68997826
Fax: (86) 10-68997826   68326333
http://www.sinolingua.com.cn
E-mail: hyjx@sinolingua.com.cn
Facebook: www.facebook.com/sinolingua
Printed by Beijing Xicheng Printing Co., Ltd

Printed in the People's Republic of China

编者的话

对于广大汉语学习者来说，要想快速提高汉语水平，扩大阅读量是很有必要的。"彩虹桥"汉语分级读物为汉语学习者提供了一系列有趣、有用的汉语阅读材料。本系列读物按照词汇量进行分级，力求用限定的词汇讲述精彩的故事。本套读物主要有以下特点：

一、分级精准，循序渐进。我们参考"新汉语水平考试（HSK）词汇表"（2012 年修订版）、《汉语国际教育用音节汉字词汇等级划分（国家标准）》和《常用汉语 1500 高频词语表》等词汇分级标准，结合《欧洲语言教学与评估框架性共同标准》（CEFR），设计了一套适合汉语学习者的"彩虹桥"词汇分级标准。本系列读物分为 7 个级别（入门级*、1 级、2 级、3 级、4 级、5 级、6 级），供不同水平的汉语学习者选择，每个级别故事的生词数量不超过本级别对应词汇量的 20%。随着级别的升高，故事的篇幅逐渐加长。本系列读物与 HSK、CEFR 的对应级别，各级词汇量以及每本书的字数详见下表。

---

* 入门级（Starter）在封底用 S 标识。

级别	入门级	1级	2级	3级	4级	5级	6级
对应级别	HSK1 CEFR A1	HSK1-2 CEFR A1-A2	HSK2-3 CEFR A2-B1	HSK3 CEFR A2-B1	HSK3-4 CEFR B1	HSK4 CEFR B1-B2	HSK5 CEFR B2-C1
词汇量	150	300	500	750	1 000	1 500	2 500
字数	1 000	2 500	5 000	7 500	10 000	15 000	25 000

二、故事精彩，题材多样。本套读物选材的标准就是"精彩"，所选的故事要么曲折离奇，要么感人至深，对读者构成奇妙的吸引力。选题广泛取材于中国的神话传说、民间故事、文学名著、名人传记和历史故事等，让汉语学习者在阅读中潜移默化地了解中国的文化和历史。

三、结构合理，实用性强。"彩虹桥"系列读物的每一本书中，除了中文故事正文之外，都配有主要人物的中英文介绍、生词英文注释及例句、故事正文的英文翻译、练习题和生词表，方便读者阅读和理解故事内容，提升汉语阅读能力。练习题主要采用客观题，题型多样，难度适中，并附有参考答案，既可供汉语教师在课堂上教学使用，又可供汉语学习者进行自我水平检测。

如果您对本系列读物有什么想法，比如推荐精彩故事、提出改进意见等，请发邮件到 liuxiaolin@sinolingua. com.cn，与我们交流探讨。也可以关注我们的微信公众号 CHQRainbowBridge，随时与我们交流互动。同时，微信公众号会不定期发布有关"彩虹桥"的出版信息，以及汉语阅读、中国文化小知识等。

韩 颖 刘小琳

Preface

For students who study Chinese as a foreign language, it's crucial for them to enlarge the scope of their reading to improve their comprehension skills. The "Rainbow Bridge" Graded Chinese Reader series is designed to provide a collection of interesting and useful Chinese reading materials. This series grades each volume by its vocabulary level and brings the learners into every scene through vivid storytelling. The series has the following features:

I. A gradual approach by grading the volumes based on vocabulary levels. We have consulted the New HSK Vocabulary (2012 Revised Edition), the *Graded Chinese Syllables, Characters and Words for the Application of Teaching Chinese to the Speakers of Other Languages (National Standard)* and the 1500 Commonly Used High Frequency Chinese Vocabulary, along with the Common European Framework of Reference for Languages (CEFR) to design the "Rainbow Bridge" vocabulary grading standard. The series is divided into seven levels (Starter*, Level 1, Level 2, Level 3, Level 4, Level 5 and Level 6) for students at different stages in their Chinese education to choose from. For each level, new words are no more than 20% of the vocabulary amount as specified in the corresponding HSK and CEFR levels.

---

* Represented by "S" on the back cover.

As the levels progress, the passage length will in turn increase. The following table indicates the corresponding "Rainbow Bridge" level, HSK and CEFR levels, the vocabulary amount, and number of characters.

Level	Starter	1	2	3	4	5	6
HSK/ CEFR Level	HSK1 CEFR A1	HSK1-2 CEFR A1-A2	HSK2-3 CEFR A2-B1	HSK3 CEFR A2-B1	HSK3-4 CEFR B1	HSK4 CEFR B1-B2	HSK5 CEFR B2-C1
Vocabulary	150	300	500	750	1,000	1,500	2,500
Characters	1,000	2,500	5,000	7,500	10,000	15,000	25,000

II. Intriguing stories on various themes. The series features engaging stories known for their twists and turns as well as deeply touching plots. The readers will find it a joyful experience to read the stories. The topics are selected from Chinese mythology, legends, folklore, literary classics, biographies of renowned people and historical tales. Such widely ranged topics would exert an invisible, yet formative, influence on readers' understanding of Chinese culture and history.

III. Reasonably structured and easy to use. For each volume of the "Rainbow Bridge" series, apart from a Chinese story, we also provide an introduction to the main characters in Chinese and English, new words with English explanations and sample sentences, and an English translation of the story, followed by comprehension exercises and a vocabulary list to help users read and understand the story and improve their Chinese reading skills. The exercises are mainly presented as objective questions that take on various forms with moderate difficulty. Moreover, keys to the exercises are also provided. The series can be used by teachers in class or by students for self-study.

If you have any questions, comments or suggestions about the series, please email us at liuxiaolin@sinolingua.com.cn. You can also exchange ideas with us via our WeChat account: CHQRainbowBridge. This account will provide updates on the series along with Chinese reading materials and cultural tips.

Han Ying and Liu Xiaolin

主要人物和地点
Main Characters and Places

沉　香 (Chénxiāng)：神仙三圣母和凡人刘彦昌的儿子。

Chenxiang:　The Son of Saint Mother, a goddess, and Liu Yan-chang, a mortal.

三圣母 (Sānshèngmǔ)：华山上的女神，凡人刘彦昌的妻子，沉香的妈妈。

Sanshengmu (Saint Mother):　The goddess who lived on Mount Hua. She was Liu Yanchang's wife and Chenxiang's mother.

刘彦昌 (Liú Yànchāng)：读书人，三圣母的丈夫，沉香的爸爸。

Liu Yanchang:　A scholar who was the husband of Saint Mother and the father of Chenxiang.

二郎神 (Èrlángshén)：神仙，三圣母的哥哥。他的额头中间多了一只眼睛。

Erlang Shen (God Erlang):　An immortal and brother of Saint Mother. He had a third eye in the middle of his forehead.

霹雳大仙 (Pīlì Dàxiān)：神仙，沉香的师父。武功高强。

Pili Daxian (God of Thunder):　An immortal with remarkable kung fu skills. He was the master of Chenxiang.

华　山 (Huà Shān)：在中国的西北边，陕西省境内。五岳之一。

Mount Hua:　Located in Shaanxi Province in China's northwest, Mount Hua is one of the five sacred mountains in China.

宝莲灯 ①

① 宝莲灯
(bǎoliándēng) *n.*
magical lotus lantern

② 凡人 (fánrén)
n. mortal
e.g., 凡人快乐地生活在大地上。

③ 神仙 (shénxiān)
n. immortal
e.g., 神仙和凡人是不可以生活在一起的。

④ 盏 (zhǎn) *m.w.*
(for lamps)
e.g., 你看！这里有一盏灯。

很多年以前，大地上不只生活着凡人 ②，还生活着神仙 ③。在华山上，就生活着一个神仙，大家都叫她三圣母。三圣母不仅长得漂亮，还很喜欢帮助人们，人们都很喜欢她。

三圣母有一盏 ④ 宝莲

1

灯。宝莲灯看起来像① 莲花② 一样，它一发光③，就有了强大④ 的力量⑤，不但能打败⑥ 凡人，也能打败神仙。三圣母用宝莲灯的力量，帮助着需要帮助的人们。

三圣母有个哥哥叫二郎神，他是一个自私⑦ 的人。二郎神见三圣母的那盏宝莲灯力量很强大，就很想抢⑧ 走它。只是他努力了很长时间，还是没能抢到它。

有一天，有个叫刘彦昌的读书人路过华山，他一看到三圣母，就爱上了她。三圣母见刘彦昌人很好，又高大英俊⑨，也很喜欢他。慢慢地，三圣母就接受了刘彦昌的爱，和他

① 像 (xiàng) v.
be like, resemble
e.g., 你看起来像是只有十八岁一样。

② 莲花 (liánhuā)
n. lotus
e.g., 等到那时候，莲花就开了。

③ 发光 (fāguāng) v.
shine, give out light
e.g., 星星在天上发光。

④ 强大 (qiángdà) adj.
strong, powerful
e.g., 这个国家很强大。

⑤ 力量 (lìliàng) n.
power, strength
e.g., 他还年轻，有的是力量。

⑥ 打败 (dǎbài) v.
defeat
e.g., 我们打败了敌人。

⑦ 自私 (zìsī) adj.
selfish
e.g., 他很自私，大家都不喜欢他。

⑧ 抢 (qiǎng) v.
snatch, grab
e.g., 你为什么要抢我的东西？

⑨ 英俊 (yīngjùn) adj.
handsome
e.g., 他是一个英俊的小伙子。

① 生 (shēng) v.
give birth to
e.g., 她生了好几个
孩子。

生活在了一起。

　　一年以后，三圣母为刘彦昌生①下了一个可爱的男孩子，这个孩子叫沉香。三圣母每天都过得很快乐。她想："我有一个这么爱我的丈夫，有一个这么可爱的儿子，我真的很幸福！"

后来，<u>二郎神</u>知道了<u>三圣母</u>和凡人结婚的事情。他想："<u>三圣母</u>这回做错了事情，应该受到惩罚①。这一次，我一定要拿到宝莲灯！"

<u>二郎神</u>找到了<u>三圣母</u>，生气地对她说："人有

① 惩罚 (chéngfá)
v. punish
e.g., 为了惩罚他，她把他关在了门外。

人的生活，神仙有神仙的生活，神仙和人是不可以在一起的！你放着好好的神仙的日子不过，一定要跟一个凡人在一起，还为他生了孩子！你每天都在想什么啊？"

三圣母听二郎神说完后，对他说："凡人怎么了？我丈夫他做事情很认真，人又很好，比很多神仙好多了。和他在一起，我很快乐。而有沉香这样一个孩子，我感到非常幸福。他让我觉得每一天都有新的希望。"

二郎神见三圣母非常爱她的孩子沉香，就冷笑着对她说："我才不关心你幸不幸福！你那么想跟凡人在一起，你就等着接受惩罚吧！"说完，他就走了。

① 救火 (jiùhuǒ) v.
put off a fire
e.g., 消防队员正在
救火。

这天晚上，二郎神让人在三圣母家放了一把火。在三圣母和刘彦昌忙着救火①的时候，二郎神把沉香抢走了。三圣母发现儿子不见了，就去找二郎神，让他放过儿子沉香。二郎神对三圣母说："你想要回沉香，可以啊。但是，你得把宝莲灯拿出来！如果你不给我，我就杀了沉香！"

三圣母回答说："只要你放了沉香，你让我做什么都可以！"说完，她小心地拿出了宝莲灯，给了二郎神。二郎神拿到宝莲灯以后，用强大的力量把三圣母压① 在了华山下。没有了宝莲灯的三圣母，从那以后再也没有出过华山。

后来，刘彦昌和沉香

① 压 (yā) v. press, weigh down e.g., 你压到我的包了。

去了一个离华山很远的地方生活。因为沉香从小和爸爸生活在一起，很多小朋友就老是说他是没妈的孩子。沉香非常难过，他每次都哭着问爸爸："爸爸，你能告诉我妈妈在哪里吗？我是不是真的没有妈妈啊？"每一次沉香问起这件事情，刘彦昌都会对他说："沉香，你还小。等你长大了，我会告诉你的。"

时间一天天过去了，沉香八岁了。有一天晚上，刘彦昌对沉香说："沉香，你已经八岁了，有些事情，是时候告诉你了。"然后，他就告诉了沉香他的妈妈是三圣母。他还告诉了沉香三圣母是怎么用宝莲灯帮助人们的，二郎神是怎么抢走宝莲灯，又是怎么把三圣母压在华山下的。

① 救 (jiù) v.
save, rescue
e.g., 哥哥跳进水里,
救出了弟弟。

　　沉香听爸爸说到妈妈为了救①他而被二郎神压在华山下以后,又是高兴又是难过。高兴的是,原来,他也有一个非常爱他的妈妈;难过的是,他的妈妈为了他而被压在华山下。他想:"不管怎么样,我都要救出我的妈妈!"

这天晚上，<u>沉香</u>做了一个和妈妈在一起的梦^①。在梦里，太阳刚刚下去，月亮出来了。他和妈妈坐着小船，在水上慢慢地前行。妈妈坐在他的旁边，快乐地唱着歌儿。水里有很多鱼，也有很多莲花。莲花有白有红，还有很多他没见过的颜色。风一来，莲花就跳起舞来，<u>沉香</u>也跟着它们跳起舞来，一会儿

① 梦 (mèng)
n. dream
e.g., 你有没有做过这样的梦？

就忘记了那些不高兴的事情。他想："和妈妈在一起，是多么幸福的事情啊！"

第二天早上，<u>沉香</u>离开了爸爸，一个人出发去找妈妈。他白天和晚上都在走，别人出门工作的时候他在走，别人回家休息了他还在走。他又累又饿，不知道过了多长时间，才走到了<u>华山</u>下。

沉香在华山下大叫着："妈妈！妈妈！"三圣母听到后，问："沉香，是你吗，我的儿子？"沉香高兴地回答说："妈妈，是我！我一定会救你出来的！"三圣母告诉沉香："要想救我出来，就得打败二郎神，拿回宝莲灯。可是，二郎神是神仙，你打不过他

① 武功 (wǔgōng) *n.*
kung fu, martial arts
e.g., 你跟谁学的武功?

② 师父 (shīfu) *n.*
master, teacher
e.g., 师父教会了他很多东西。

的。"沉香问妈妈："那我怎么做才能打得过他?"三圣母回答说："你可以去找霹雳大仙学习武功①，他会帮助你的。"

就这样，沉香离开了妈妈，去找霹雳大仙。他一边走一边打听，又不知道过了多长时间，他才找到了霹雳大仙。沉香请霹雳大仙当他的师父②。霹雳大仙见他不过是个八岁的小孩子，一开始不愿意。后来，他看沉香在他门前不走，一定要跟着他学习，他也就同意了当沉香的师父。

　　沉香认真地学习武功，从不觉得累。他想："只要我努力地学习武功，就可

以打败二郎神，救出妈妈了！"不管是雨天还是雪天，不管是天冷还是天热，沉香都坚持每天跟着师父学习武功。有时候，他想玩一会儿，但又会想起小朋友们说他没有妈妈，想起妈妈为了他而被压在华山下，想起他做的和妈妈一起坐船的梦……这个时候，沉香就会对着华山的方向说："妈妈，对不起。我以后不再想玩的事情了。我会认真地学习武功，救您出来的！"

一年又一年过去了，沉香十六岁的生日到了。他对霹雳大仙说："师父，我已经跟您学习了八年的武功，谢谢您这八年来每

天教我武功，还对我这么
好。现在，我要离开您，
去救我的妈妈去了。"霹雳
大仙对沉香说："沉香，你
武功已经学习得差不多了，
是时候去救你妈妈出来了。
我这里有一把开山神斧①，你
可以拿着它去救你的妈妈。"

　沉香离开了师父，去
救他的妈妈。他先去了华
山，想用师父给他的开山

③ 开山神斧 (kāishān shénfǔ) n. sacred ax for cutting into a mountain

① 砍 (kǎn) *v.*
cut, chop
e.g., 你把它砍坏了
怎么办?

神斧把华山砍①开。可是，虽然沉香已经学习了八年的武功，但还是砍不开华山，只是砍下了一点花花草草。他想："如果这样砍下去，不知道要砍到什么时候才能救出妈妈。"这时候，他想到了妈妈八年前对他说过的话，"要想救我出来，就得打败二郎神，

拿回宝莲灯。"他决定去找
二郎神，拿回宝莲灯。

　　沉香到了二郎神家里，
请二郎神把宝莲灯还给他。
二郎神见沉香才不过十六
岁，哪里会愿意把宝莲灯
给他。沉香见二郎神不给
他，就上前跟二郎神打了
起来。他们打啊打，从天
上打到地上，又从地上打
到水里。从太阳出来打到

① 血 (xuè) *n.* blood e.g., 人的血和鱼的血颜色一样吗?

太阳下去，又打到太阳再次出来。

二郎神见这么打下去打不败沉香，就拿出了宝莲灯。宝莲灯发起光来，和沉香在梦里见过的莲花一样好看。沉香被重重地打倒在地上。他的身体上和衣服上都是血①，他觉得他快要死了。

沉香又开始做梦了。在梦里，他还是和妈妈在一起，妈妈唱着歌儿，他跟着莲花一起跳着舞。小船在水上前行，鱼也在跟着他们前行。他是多么想要和妈妈在一起啊，可是现在他要离开这个世界了。想到这里，他的眼泪①就流②下来了。

① 眼泪 (yǎnlèi) *n.* tear
e.g., 他很难过，脸上都是眼泪。

② 流 (liú) *v.* flow
e.g., 水从西边流到了东边。

22

① 奇迹 (qíjì)
n. miracle
e.g., 你相信奇迹吗?

这时候，奇迹①出现了。那些眼泪，都离开了<u>沉香</u>的身体，跑到了宝莲灯旁边。它们变成了红的和白的莲花，在宝莲灯的旁边跳起舞来。宝莲灯离开了<u>二郎神</u>，又一次发起光来。这些光一起跑啊跑，最后都跑进了<u>沉香</u>的身体里。

沉香<u>醒</u>①了过来。他见身体上和衣服上的血都不见了，就明白了他已经得到了宝莲灯的力量。<u>沉香</u>站了起来，一下子就把<u>二郎神</u>打倒在地上。<u>二郎神</u>见<u>沉香</u>得到了宝莲灯的力量，知道打不过他，就很快地跑走了。

① 醒 (xǐng) v.
wake up
e.g., 我们要出发了，快醒一醒！

沉香拿起宝莲灯，又回到华山。他再一次拿起开山神斧，向华山砍去。这一次，华山一下子就被砍成了两半，三圣母被救了出来。沉香拿着宝莲灯和开山神斧，和三圣母一起回家了。从那以后，他们一家三口一起快快乐乐地生活了下去。

二郎神被沉香打跑以后，就想啊想，他怎么也想不明白："为什么眼泪可以帮助沉香得到宝莲灯的力量呢？"霹雳大仙告诉他："那是爱，而不只是眼泪。爱是这个世界上最强大的力量，爱是不会被打败的。不管有没有宝莲灯，只要有爱在，就会有坚持。有了坚持，沉香最后都会救出他的妈妈。"

Magical Lotus Lantern

Many years ago, human beings were not alone on earth since immortals also resided here. Sanshengmu, also known as Saint Mother, was a beautiful goddess who lived on Mount Hua. She was always eager to help, and the people liked her very much.

Saint Mother had a magical lotus lantern which looked like a lotus flower. The lantern became extremely powerful once it glowed. It had the power to defeat both mortals and immortals. Using the power of the lotus lantern, Saint Mother helped those in need.

Saint Mother had an elder brother, God Erlang. He was very selfish. Knowing the enormous power of the lotus lantern, he wanted to take it for himself. He tried many times over a long period, but still couldn't get it.

One day, a scholar named Liu Yanchang passed by Mount Hua. Liu fell in love with Saint Mother at first sight. Saint Mother also grew very fond of Liu as the days passed by because he was such a nice person, not to mention he was tall and handsome. After some time, they started to live together.

One year after that, Saint Mother gave birth to a lovely baby boy. They named him Chenxiang. Saint Mother found joy in each day. She said to herself, "I have a husband who loves me so dearly and a son who is so adorable. I'm a very happy

27

woman indeed!"

Afterwards, God Erlang learned of Saint Mother's marriage. He thought, "Saint Mother broke the rules by marrying a mortal. She should to be punished. This time, I will get the lotus lantern!"

God Erlang found Saint Mother and said to her angrily, "Human beings have a life of their own, so do the immortals. Immortals and humans can't live together! You should have cherished your life as an immortal. Why would you marry a human and deliver a son for him? I don't know what was going on in your mind."

Hearing God Erlang's accusations, Saint Mother replied, "What's wrong with being a human? My husband is a kind person who cares about what he does. He is much better than some immortals. I'm happy living with him. My son Chenxiang makes me a happy mother and brings me hope every single day."

God Erlang noticed that Saint Mother loved her son deeply. He said to her with a sneer, "It's none of my business whether you are happy or not! Since you want to live with mortals so much, you will receive your punishment in due time!" With that, he left.

That night, God Erlang sent people to set Saint Mother's house on fire. When Saint Mother and Liu Yancheng were busy putting off the fire, God Erlang kidnapped baby Chenxiang. When Saint Mother found out her son had been taken away, she went to see God Erlang and asked him to free her son. God Erlang said to Saint Mother, "You can have Chenxiang back, but you will have to trade your lotus lantern. Without the lantern, I will kill Chenxiang!"

Saint Mother replied, "As long as you release Chenxiang, I will do whatever you want!" Then, she carefully took out the lotus lantern and handed it to God Erlang. Grabbing the lantern, God Erlang used magical powers to imprison Saint Mother under Mount Hua. Saint Mother's power was greatly weakened without the lotus lantern so she was forced to stay under the mountain.

Later, Liu Yanchang and Chenxiang moved not very far from Mount Hua. Since Chenxiang lived with only his dad, many of his friends called him a motherless child. Chenxiang became very upset. He would cry and ask his father, "Dad, could you tell me where my mom is? Am I a motherless child?" Every time Chenxiang brought this up, Liu Yanchang would say to him, "Chenxiang, you are still young. I will tell you what happened when you grow up."

Years passed and Chenxiang turned eight. One evening, Liu Yanchang said to him, "Chenxiang, since you are old enough, it's time to tell you what happened to your mother." He told Chenxiang that his mother was Saint Mother who used the lotus lantern to help people. He also told him how God Erlang grabbed the lantern and imprisoned his mother under Mount Hua.

Chenxiang had mixed feelings when he heard his mother was imprisoned by God Erlang when she tried to save him. Chenxiang felt happy because to his relief, he had a mother who loved him so much, yet, he felt so sad because his mother was still under the mountain. He said to himself, "No matter what, I will save my mother!"

On that very night, Chenxiang had a dream in which he and his mother were together. In his dream, the sun just set and the moon rose. He and his mother were on a boat which was traveling slowly in the water. His mother was singing happily sitting beside him. There were many fish as well as many lotuses in the water. The lotuses were white, red and many other colors he had never seen. When the wind blew, the lotuses danced with the wind. Chenxiang also joined them in their dance and forgot all the unhappy stuff. He thought, "What a happy thing it is to be with mom!"

The next morning, Chenxiang left his father and set off to find his mother on his own. Day and night, he continued to travel. When people started work, he was trekking; when people returned home to rest, he was still trekking. Hungry and exhausted, he finally made it to the foot of Mount Hua without knowing how long he had traveled.

At the foot of Mount Hua, Chenxiang shouted, "Mom! Mom!" Hearing his cry, Saint Mother asked, "Is that you, Chenxiang, my son?" Chenxiang gladly replied, "Mom, it's me! I will rescue you from this place!" Saint Mother told him, "To rescue me, you need to defeat God Erlang and get the lotus lantern back, but God Erlang is an immortal, you can't beat him."

Chenxiang asked her, "What can I do to defeat him?" Saint Mother said, "Go to find the God of Thunder and learn kung fu from him. He will help you."

Chenxiang then left his mom and went to search for the God of Thunder. He went to different places to inquire the whereabouts of the god and finally found him after quite some time. Chenxiang asked him to be his master. The God of Thunder saw Chenxiang was only a young child of eight years old, so he didn't want to teach him at first. However, Chenxiang was determined to learn from him. Chenxiang waited in front of the gate of his house and refused to leave. Finally, the God of Thunder agreed to take Chenxiang as his pupil.

Chenxiang was very serious about learning kung fu. He never felt tired. He thought, "If I can work hard to learn kung fu, I will defeat God Erlang and rescue my mom!" In spite of the rain or snow, hot or cold, Chenxiang never stopped practicing kung fu, not even for one day. Sometimes, when he really wanted to play for a while, he would think of being a motherless child as his friends said and think of his mother who was still under Mount Hua because of him. He would think of his dream in which he and his mother were on a boat... Then, Chenxiang would face the direction of Mount Hua and say, "Mom, I'm sorry. I won't think of playing anymore. I will practice kung fu diligently and rescue you!"

Years passed by, and Chenxiang celebrated his sixteenth birthday. He said to the God of Thunder, "Master, I have been learning kung fu from you for eight years. Thank you for teaching me and for being so kind to me. Now, I have to leave you to rescue my mom." The God of Thunder said to him, "Chenxiang, you've learned enough kung fu and it's time to rescue your mom. Here is a sacred ax that can cut into a mountain. You can use it to free your mom."

Chenxiang then left his master and set off to rescue his mom. He went to Mount Hua first and intended to cut open the mountain using the sacred ax. Although he practiced kung fu for eight years, he could only cut down some trees and grass and the mountain was still intact. He thought, "It would take ages to save my mother if I continue to cut things like this." At that moment, his mother's words rang out, "To rescue me, you need to defeat God Erlang and get the lotus lantern back." So he decided to find God Erlang and get back the lantern.

Chenxiang went to the home of God Erlang and asked to have the lotus lantern back. Knowing Chenxiang was only 16 years old, God Erlang certainly didn't want to give the lantern to him. Chenxiang had to fight God Erlang for the lantern. They fought in the sky, on earth and then in the water. They fought from sunrise to sunset and then to another sunrise.

God Erlang realized that he couldn't defeat Chenxiang. So he took out the lotus lantern. The lantern started to glow. It was as beautiful as the lotuses in Chenxiang's dream. Chenxiang was hit severely and fell to the ground. His body and clothes were covered in blood. Chenxiang thought he was dying.

Chenxiang then fell into another dream in which he was still with his mother. His mother was singing and he was dancing with the lotuses. The boat was moving in the water with the fish accompanying them. How much he desired to be with his mother, but now he was about to die. Thinking of that, tears rolled down his face.

Right then, a miracle happened. The tears flew away from Chenxiang and made their way to the lotus lantern. They became red and white lotuses and danced by the lantern. The lantern then drifted away from God Erlang and started to glow again. Beams of light flew into Chenxiang's body.

Chenxiang woke up. He noticed that the blood on his body and clothes all dispeared, and realized that he had gained the lotus lantern's power. Chenxiang stood up and knocked God Erlang down with one strike. God Erlang knew he couldn't defeat Chenxiang, who had already acquired the power of the lantern. So he didn't waste time and fled.

Chenxiang picked up the lotus lantern and returned to Mount Hua. Again he used the sacred ax to cut the mountain. This time, Mount Hua was cut in half. Saint Mother was finally free! Taking the lantern and the sacred ax with him, Chenxiang went home with Saint Mother. From then on, the three of them lived happily together.

God Erlang was defeated by Chenxiang, but he could never figure out why tears could help Chenxiang to acquire the power of the lotus lantern. The God of Thunder told him the reason, "It's love, not the tears. Love is the most powerful thing in the world, and love cannot be conquered. With or without the lotus lantern, when there is love, there will be determination and persistence. With determination, Chenxiang would rescue his mother eventually."

一、选择题。 Choose the correct answer.

1. 沉香姓什么? (　　)

A. 沉　　　　B. 刘　　　　C. 二　　　　D. 三

2. 沉香家里有几个人? (　　)

A. 一个　　　B. 两个　　　C. 三个　　　D. 四个

3. 二郎神是三圣母的什么人? (　　)

A. 爸爸　　　B. 儿子　　　C. 哥哥　　　D. 丈夫

4. 和刘彦昌在一起, 三圣母觉得怎么样? (　　)

A. 很快乐　　B. 很生气　　C. 很难过　　D. 很无聊

5. 宝莲灯看起来像什么一样? (　　)

A. 太阳　　　B. 月亮　　　C. 雪花　　　D. 莲花

6. 小朋友们说沉香是没妈的孩子, 沉香觉得怎么样? (　　)

A. 难过　　　B. 高兴　　　C. 认真　　　D. 幸福

7. 沉香的梦里没有什么? (　　)

A. 妈妈　　　B. 爸爸　　　C. 小鱼　　　D. 小船

8. 在沉香几岁的时候, 爸爸告诉了他妈妈的事情? (　　)

A. 五岁　　　B. 七岁　　　C. 八岁　　　D. 十岁

9. 沉香跟着霹雳大仙学习了几年的武功？（　　　）

　　A. 六年　　　　B. 八年　　　C. 十年　　　D. 三年

10. 沉香得到了什么的力量之后，才救出了妈妈？（　　　）

　　A. 开山神斧　　　　　　　B. 二郎神

　　C. 霹雳大仙　　　　　　　D. 宝莲灯

二、判断题：请根据故事内容判断下列说法是否正确，如果正确请标"T"，不正确请标"F"。
Decide whether the following statements are true (T) or false (F).

1. 人们非常喜欢三圣母。　　　　　　　　　　（　　　）

2. 三圣母和刘彦昌一起住在华山下。　　　　　（　　　）

3. 二郎神很关心三圣母，他对她很好。　　　　（　　　）

4. 二郎神先抢走了宝莲灯，然后在三圣母家放了一把火。

　　　　　　　　　　　　　　　　　　　　　（　　　）

5. 三圣母被二郎神压在了华山下。　　　　　　（　　　）

6. 沉香和爸爸一起去华山救妈妈。　　　　　　（　　　）

7. 沉香还没救出妈妈，就离开了这个世界。　　（　　　）

8. 沉香为了救妈妈而去学习武功。　　　　　　（　　　）

9. 沉香最后打跑了二郎神，拿到了宝莲灯。　　（　　　）

10. 沉香救出妈妈以后，回去和师父霹雳大仙一起生活了。

　　　　　　　　　　　　　　　　　　　　　（　　　）

1. 很多年以前，大地上不只生活着（　　　），还生活着神仙。在华山上，就生活着一个神仙，大家都叫她三圣母。三圣母不仅长得（　　　），还很喜欢帮助人们，人们都很（　　　）她。三圣母有一盏宝莲灯。宝莲灯看起来像（　　　）一样，它一（　　　），就有了强大的力量，不但能打败凡人，也能打败（　　　）。

　　A. 莲花　　　　B. 喜欢　　　　C. 凡人

　　D. 发光　　　　E. 神仙　　　　F. 漂亮

2. 沉香和妈妈（　　　）着小船，在水上慢慢地前行。妈妈坐在他的旁边，快乐地（　　　）着歌儿。水里有很多鱼，也有很多莲花。莲花有白有红，还有很多他没（　　　）过的颜色。风一来，莲花就（　　　）起舞来，沉香也跟着它们跳起舞来，一会儿就（　　　）了那些不高兴的事情。他（　　　）："和妈妈在一起，是多么幸福的事情啊！"

　　A. 唱　　　　B. 跳　　　　C. 坐

　　D. 忘记　　　　E. 想　　　　F. 见

3. 这时候，奇迹（　　）了。那些眼泪，都（　　）了沉香的身体，跑到了宝莲灯旁边。它们（　　）了红的和白的莲花，在宝莲灯的旁边（　　）起舞来。宝莲灯离开了二郎神，又一次发起光来。这些光一起跑啊跑，最后都跑进了沉香的身体里。沉香（　　）了过来。他见身体上和衣服上的血都不见了，就（　　）了他已经得到了宝莲灯的力量。

A. 变成　　　B. 跳　　　　C. 醒

D. 离开　　　E. 出现　　　F. 明白

四、连线题。 Match.

1. 请为下列词语选择合适的搭配。

A. 生　　　　　　　　a. 幸福

B. 流　　　　　　　　b. 孩子

C. 感到　　　　　　　c. 眼泪

D. 受到　　　　　　　d. 漂亮

E. 长得　　　　　　　e. 惩罚

2. 根据故事内容为下列事物选择各自的特征。

A. 时间　　　　　　　　a. 幸福的

B. 个子　　　　　　　　b. 高大的

C. 力量　　　　　　　　c. 强大的

D. 事情　　　　　　　　d. 很长的

五、请根据故事内容给下列句子排列顺序。
Put the following statements in order according to the story.

A. 沉香得到了宝莲灯的力量。他站了起来，一下子就把二郎神打倒了。

B. 沉香离开了妈妈，去找霹雳大仙学习武功。

C. 沉香再一次拿起开山神斧，向华山砍去。这一次，华山一下子被砍成了两半，他的妈妈被救了出来。

D. 沉香从小和爸爸生活在一起，很多小朋友就老是说他是没妈的孩子。

E. 沉香离开霹雳大仙，到了二郎神家里，和二郎神打了起来，他被二郎神重重地打倒在地上。

F. 听爸爸说了妈妈为了救他而被二郎神压在华山下以后，沉香离开了爸爸，一个人出发去找妈妈。

G. 妈妈告诉沉香：“要想救我出来，就得打败二郎神，拿回宝莲灯。”

1. 请根据图片说说这幅图应该放在这本书的第（　　　　）页。

2. 图片中有哪些人物?

3. 图中的人物心情怎么样?

4. 他们的心情为什么会是这样的?

5. 请你用中文或英文给这幅图加一个简单的标题说明。

练习题答案 Keys to the exercises

一、选择题
1. B   2. C   3. C   4. A   5. D
6. A   7. B   8. C   9. B   10. D

二、判断题：请根据故事内容判断下列说法是否正确，
  如果正确请标 "T"，不正确请标 "F"
1. T   2. F   3. F   4. F   5. T
6. F   7. F   8. T   9. T   10. F

三、选择填空题
1. C   F   B   A   D   E
1. D   H   A   F   B   G   E   C
1. E   D   A   B   C   A   F

四、连线题
1. A-b, B-c, C-a, D-e, E-d
2. A-d, B-b, C-c, D-a

五、请根据故事内容给下列句子排列顺序
D-F-G-B-E-A-C

宝莲灯	*n.*	bǎoliándēng	magical lotus lantern
惩罚	*v.*	chéngfá	punish
发光	*v.*	fāguāng	shine, give out light
凡人	*n.*	fánrén	mortal
华山	*n.*	Huà Shān	Mount Hua
救火	*v.*	jiùhuǒ	put off a fire
开山神斧	*n.*	kāishān shénfǔ	sacred ax for cutting into a mountain
砍	*v.*	kǎn	cut, chop
泪	*n.*	lèi	tear
力量	*n.*	lìliàng	power, strength
莲花	*n.*	liánhuā	lotus
流	*v.*	liú	flow
梦	*n.*	mèng	dream
奇迹	*n.*	qíjì	miracle
强	*adj.*	qiáng	strong, powerful
抢	*v.*	qiǎng	snatch, grab
神仙	*n.*	shénxiān	immortal
生	*v.*	shēng	give birth to
师父	*n.*	shīfu	master, teacher
武功	*n.*	wǔgōng	kung fu, martial arts
像	*v.*	xiàng	be like, resemble
醒	*v.*	xǐng	wake up
血	*n.*	xuè	blood
压	*v.*	yā	press, weigh down
英俊	*adj.*	yīngjùn	handsome
盏	*m.w.*	zhǎn	(for lamps)
自私	*adj.*	zìsī	selfish

英目策划：刘小琳　韩　颖
责任编辑：刘小琳
英文翻译：张　乐
英文编辑：薛彧威
英文审订：黄长奇
封面设计：E·T创意工作室

图书在版编目（CIP）数据

宝莲灯：汉、英／刘菊改编．— 北京：华语教学
出版社，2016
（"彩虹桥"汉语分级读物．一级：300 词）
ISBN 978-7-5138-0989-4

Ⅰ．①宝… Ⅱ．①刘… Ⅲ．①汉语－对外汉语教学－
语言读物 Ⅳ．① H195.5

中国版本图书馆CIP数据核字（2015）第 155709 号

宝莲灯

刘　菊　改编

*

©华语教学出版社有限责任公司

华语教学出版社有限责任公司出版

（中国北京百万庄大街24号　邮政编码 100037）

电话：(86)10-68320585　68997826

传真：(86)10-68997826　68326333

网址：www.sinolingua.com.cn

电子信箱：hyjx@sinolingua.com.cn

新浪微博地址：http://weibo.com/sinolinguavip

北京玺诚印务有限公司印刷

2016年（32开）第1版

2017年第1版第2次印刷

（汉英）

ISBN 978-7-5138-0989-4

定价：15.00元